Plant Base Re
Health

A Handful of Quick, Delicious Recipes for Your Plant Based Meals

Tanya Lang

By reading this document, the reader agrees that under no circumstances is the author responsible for any losses, direct or indirect, which are incurred as a result of the use of information contained within this document, including, but not limited to, — errors, omissions, or inaccuracies.

TABLE OF CONTENT

Baked Beans with Mustard

• Preparation Time: 05 minutes | Cooking Time: 15 minutes | Servings: 2

Ingredients:
- ½ cup kidney beans rinsed and drained
- ½ cup pinto beans rinsed and drained
- ½ cup chickpea beans rinsed and drained
- 1 cup of water
- 1/2 cup tomato paste
- 1 teaspoon honey
- ½ tablespoon ground mustard
- 1 teaspoon paprika

Directions:
• Add the kidney beans, pinto beans, chickpeas beans, water, tomato paste, honey, ground mustard, and paprika. Lock the lid into place and turn the valve to —Sealing. ‖ Select Manual or Pressure Cook and adjust the pressure to High.
• Set the time for 8 minutes. When cooking ends, let the pressure release naturally for 15 minutes, then turn the valve to —Venting‖ to quickly release the remaining pressure. Unlock and remove the lid and stir well before serving.

Nutrition:
• Calories 268, Total Fat 2. 7g, Saturated Fat 0. 3g, Cholesterol 0mg, Sodium 555mg, Total Carbohydrate 50. 6g, Dietary Fiber 13g, Total Sugars 11. 8g, Protein 14g

Rosemary Lentils, Beans Curry

• Preparation Time: 10 minutes | Cooking Time: 30 minutes | Servings: 2

Ingredients:
- 1 cup of water
- ½ cup of brown rice
- ½ cup brown lentils
- ½ cup navy beans pre-soaked or quick-soaked
- ½ tablespoon rosemary
- 1 teaspoon garlic powder
- ½ cup chopped onions
- ½ cup low sodium vegetable broth

Directions:
- In your Instant Pot, sauté the onions in the vegetable broth and garlic powder. First, heat the broth on medium and statue the onion for about 4 minutes until translucent then add the garlic powder for another 30 seconds.
- Add the rest of the ingredients to Instant Pot, and stir it well.
- Close the lid, and seal the vent Instant Pot. Set the cooker for 23 minutes, and cook at High pressure on the Manual setting.
- Release the pressure naturally.
- Serve and season as desired.

Nutrition:
- Calories 269, Total Fat 1. 6g, Saturated Fat 0. 3g, Cholesterol 0mg, Sodium 255mg, Total Carbohydrate 55. 2g, Dietary Fiber 7. 4g, Total

Sugars 1. 6g, Protein 9. 9g

Fava Beans

- Preparation Time: 15 minutes | Cooking Time: 30 minutes | Servings: 2

Ingredients:
- 1 teaspoon olive oil
- 1 small onion, chopped
- 1 tomato, chopped
- 1 tablespoon tomato paste
- 1 cup of water
- ½ cup fava beans, drained
- ½ tablespoon ground cumin
- 1/2 teaspoons salt
- 1 1/2 teaspoons ground black pepper
- ½ teaspoon ground red pepper
- 1 tablespoon finely chopped parsley

Directions:

- In your Instant Pot, sauté olive oil and add onions. Cook and stir for 2 minutes. Add chopped tomatoes and tomato paste; cook until tomatoes are mushy, about 4 minutes.
- Pour fava beans into Instant Pot. Add 1 cup water, cumin, salt, black pepper, and ground red pepper; stir well. Close the lid, and seal the vent Instant Pot. Set the cooker for 23 minutes, and cook at High pressure on the Manual setting.
- Release the pressure naturally.
- Stir in parsley.

Nutrition:

• Calories 186, Total Fat 3. 5g, Saturated Fat 0. 5g, Cholesterol 0mg, Sodium 602mg, Total Carbohydrate 29. 9g, Dietary Fiber 11. 6g, Total Sugars 5. 5g, Protein 11. 4g

Spinach Split Pigeon Pea

- Preparation Time: 15 minutes | Cooking Time: 15 minutes | Servings: 2

Ingredients:
- ½ cup split pigeon pea
- 1 cup spinach chopped
- ½ tablespoon vegetable oil
- ¼ teaspoon cumin seeds
- 1 green chili pepper sliced (optional
- ¼ teaspoon ginger powder
- ½ teaspoon garlic powder
- 1 tomato large, chopped
- 2 cups of water
- ¼ teaspoon garam masala
- ¼ teaspoon salt
- 1/8 teaspoon turmeric powder
- 1/4 teaspoon red chili powder

Directions:

- Start the Instant Pot in Sauté mode and heat vegetable oil in it. Add cumin seeds, green chili, ginger powder, and garlic powder.
- Sauté for 30 seconds until garlic turns golden brown, then add chopped tomatoes and spices.
- Add the split pigeon pea and water. Stir well. Press Cancel and close the Instant Pot lid with the vent in the Sealing position.
- Press Manual or Pressure Cook mode for 3 minutes. When the Instant Pot beeps, do a Quick

Pressure Release.
- Open the lid and add chopped spinach and garam masala. Press Sauté mode. simmer for 2 minutes until the dal starts boiling and spinach is mixed with the lentils.
- Spinach split pigeon pea is ready to be served.

Nutrition:
- Calories 240, Total Fat 4. 8g, Saturated Fat 1g, Cholesterol 0mg, Sodium 325mg, Total Carbohydrate 38. 8g, Dietary Fiber 4. 5g, Total Sugars 5. 8g, Protein 13. 4g

Mexican Beans

- Preparation Time: 15 minutes | Cooking Time: 35 minutes | Servings: 2

Ingredients:
- ½ cup dried pinto beans
- 2 cups of water
- 1 small onion, chopped
- 1 medium ripe tomato, chopped
- 1 fresh bell pepper, chopped
- 1 tablespoon fresh cilantro, chopped

Directions:
- Select the High Sauté setting on the Instant Pot and add pinto beans, water, onion, ripe tomato, and bell pepper. Secure the lid and set the Pressure Release to Sealing. Press the Cancel button to reset the cooking program, then select the Pressure Cook or Manual setting and set the cooking time for 35 minutes at High Pressure.
- Let the pressure release naturally; this will take 10 to 20 minutes.
- Garnish with fresh cilantro.

Nutrition:
- Calories 212, Total Fat 0. 9g, Saturated Fat 0. 1g, Cholesterol 0mg, Sodium 19mg, Total Carbohydrate 40. 4g, Dietary Fiber 9. 8g, Total Sugars 7. 1g, Protein 11. 9g

Beans and Greens

• Preparation Time: 10 minutes | Cooking Time: 35 minutes | Servings: 2

Ingredients:
- 2 cups vegetable broth
- ½ cup chopped spinach
- 1 cup red kidney beans
- ½ cup black beans
- ¼ cup pinto beans,
- ¼ cup chickpeas
- 1 tablespoon butter
- ¼ tablespoon garlic powder
- Salt to taste black pepper to taste

Directions:

• Place broth and spinach into Instant Pot, and cook for 5 minutes, or until spinach is wilted.

Mix in red kidney beans, black beans, chickpea and pinto beans and liquid, and butter. Season with garlic powder, salt, and black pepper. Secure the lid and set the Pressure Release to Sealing. Press the Cancel button to reset the cooking program, then select the Pressure Cook or Manual setting and set the cooking time for 30 minutes at high pressure.

• Let the pressure release naturally; this will take 10 to 20 minutes.
Nutrition:
• Calories 372, Total Fat 5. 3g, Saturated Fat 2. 3g, Cholesterol 8mg, Sodium 416mg, Total

Carbohydrate 59. 4g, Dietary Fiber 14. 9g, Total Sugars 3. 6g, Protein

Soybean, Lentil, and Zucchini Curry

• Preparation Time: 10 minutes | Cooking Time: 15 minutes | Servings: 2

Ingredients:
- ¼ tablespoon vegetable oil
- 1 cup finely chopped onions
- ¼ tablespoon curry paste
- 2 cups vegetable broth
- ½ cup finely chopped zucchini
- ½ tablespoon ginger powder
- 1/8 teaspoon ground red pepper
- 1 teaspoon garlic powder
- ½ cup dried small red lentils
- ½ cup yellow soybeans, rinsed and drained
- 1 tablespoon minced fresh parsley
- ¼ teaspoon salt
- ¼ teaspoon freshly ground black pepper
- 2 tablespoons plain fat-free yogurt
- Fresh coriander

Directions:
• Press Sauté to preheat the Instant Pot. When the word "Hot" appears on the display, add the vegetable oil and sauté the onions for about 5 minutes, until the onions are translucent. Stir curry paste; cook for 1 minute. Add 1/2 cup broth, zucchini, ginger powder, red pepper, and garlic

powder; cook 5 minutes or until zucchini is tender, stirring occasionally.
- Add the remaining broth, lentils, and soybeans.
- Lock the lid in place. Press Manual and adjust to 4 minutes of cooking time.
- When the beep sounds, quickly release the pressure by pressing Cancel and twist the steam handle to the Venting position.
- Stir in cilantro, salt, and black pepper. Garnish with coriander leaves and yogurt, if desired.

Nutrition:
- Calories 373, Total Fat 10g, Saturated Fat 1. 6g, Cholesterol 1mg, Sodium 1089mg, Total Carbohydrate 47g, Dietary Fiber 9. 5g, Total Sugars 6g, Protein 26. 5g

Spicy Navy Bean and Chard

Ingredients:
- ½ tablespoon vegetable oil
- ¼ cup onions chopped
- 1 teaspoon garlic powder
- 2 cups vegetable broth
- 1 cup dried navy beans
- ½ cup chard stems removed, leaves sliced
- 1/8 teaspoon paprika
- 1/8 teaspoon sea salt

Directions:
- Press Sauté to preheat the Instant pot. When the word "Hot" appears on the display, add the vegetable oil and sauté the onions and garlic powder for about 5 minutes, until the onions are translucent.
- Add the navy beans and continue to stir. Stir in the first 2 cups of vegetable broth.
- Lock the lid in place. Press Manual and adjust to 10 minutes of cooking time.
- When the beep sounds, quickly release the pressure by pressing Cancel and twisting the steam handle to the Venting position.
- Press Sauté and stir chopped green chard.
- Cook, stirring constantly until the chard has wilted about 2 minutes.

• Taste and add salt if you think it's needed, and pinch more paprika, if you like more spice.

Nutrition:
• Calories 191, Total Fat 5. 8g, Saturated Fat 1. 1g, Cholesterol 0mg, Sodium 1190mg, Total Carbohydrate 23. 7g, Dietary Fiber 7. 6g, Total Sugars 2. 8g, Protein 12. 4g

Carrot and Soy Bean Stir Fry

- Preparation Time: 15 minutes | Cooking Time: 20 minutes | Servings: 2

Ingredients:
- ¼ cup cauliflower florets
- ¼ cup broccoli florets
- 1/2 cup dried soybeans
- 1 large carrot, chopped
- ½ cup vegetable broth
- 1 tablespoon butter
- 1 onion, chopped
- ½ cup pumpkin, sliced
- 2 large mushrooms, sliced
- 1 tablespoon garlic powder
- Salt and pepper to taste
- Select the Sauté setting on the Instant Pot, add the butter, and heat for 1 minute. Add the

onions, carrots, garlic powder, salt, pumpkin, broccoli, cauliflower, and mushrooms. Sauté for about 10 minutes, until the vegetables give up some of their liquid and begin to brown just a bit.

- Add vegetable broth and soybeans.
- Lock the lid into place. Select Pressure Cook or Manual, and adjust the pressure to High and the

time to 12 minutes. After cooking, let the pressure release naturally for 10 minutes, then quickly release any remaining pressure.
- Unlock the lid.
- Taste the soybeans and adjust the seasoning.
- Serve and enjoy.

Nutrition:
- Calories 291, Total Fat 5. 2g, Saturated Fat 3. 1g, Cholesterol 0mg, Sodium 1089mg, Total Carbohydrate 13. 7g, Dietary Fiber 4. 6g, Total Sugars 1g, Protein 22. 4g

Tomato Chickpeas Curry

• Preparation Time: 15 minutes | Cooking Time: 20 minutes | Servings: 2

Ingredients:
- 1 tablespoon avocado oil
- 5 tomatoes, cored and diced
- 1 1/2 teaspoons garlic powder
- ½ tablespoon coarsely chopped fresh rosemary
- 1½ cups chickpeas drained and rinsed
- ½ teaspoon kosher salt
- Freshly ground black pepper
- 3 cups of water

Directions:
- Select the Sauté setting on the Instant Pot, add the avocado oil. Add the tomatoes and sauté for about 3 minutes until they start to break down and tomatoes become saucy. Add the garlic powder, rosemary and sauté for 1 minute more.
- Add water and chickpeas, salt, and pepper.
- Lock the lid into place. Select Pressure Cook or Manual, and adjust the pressure to High and the time to 12 minutes. After cooking, let the pressure release naturally for 10 minutes, then quickly release any remaining pressure.
- Unlock the lid.
- Serve and enjoy.

Nutrition:

• Calories 434, Total Fat 7. 6g, Saturated Fat 0. 9g, Cholesterol 0mg, Sodium 621mg, Total Carbohydrate 74. 1g, Dietary Fiber 21. 6g, Total Sugars 19. 2g, Protein 22. 4g

Lemony Lentil and Greens

Ingredients:
- ½ cup brown lentils, rinsed
- ½ tablespoon butter
- 1 onion, diced
- ½ cup kale, chopped
- 2 cups vegetable broth
- Juice of 1 lemon
- 1/4 teaspoon paprika

Directions:

• Select the Sauté setting on the Instant Pot, add the butter, onions, sprinkle with a pinch of sea salt, and cook for 1 minute.
• Next, add the chopped kale and paprika then stir together. Cook for another 2 minutes until the kale is slightly soft. Add the brown lentils to the Instant Pot along with the vegetable broth.
• Lock the lid into place. Select Pressure Cook or Manual, and adjust the pressure to High and the time to 20 minutes. After cooking, let the pressure release naturally for 10 minutes, then quickly release any remaining pressure. Unlock the lid.
• Squeeze the juice of a lemon into the pot and stir together.

Nutrition:
• Calories 264, Total Fat 4. 9g, Saturated Fat 2. 3g, Cholesterol 8mg, Sodium 798mg, Total

Carbohydrate 36. 8g, Dietary Fiber 16. 2g, Total Sugars 4g, Protein 18. 4g

Moroccan Red Lentil Curry

• Preparation Time: 10 minutes | Cooking Time: 30 minutes | Servings: 2

Ingredients:
- ½ cup dry red lentils
- ½ leek, diced
- 1 small onion, diced
- ½ zucchini, peeled and chopped
- 1 potato, peeled and chopped
- ½ teaspoon garlic powder
- 1 tablespoon coconut oil
- ½ teaspoon cumin
- ½ teaspoon turmeric powder
- ¼ teaspoon coriander powder
- ¼ teaspoon nutmeg
- 2 cups vegetable broth
- Juice of ½ lemon
- Salt to taste (if needed
- Fresh cilantro for topping
- Select Sauté and adjust to Normal or Medium heat. Add the coconut oil to the Instant Pot and

heat until shimmering. Add onions and the leeks. Cook for 2 minutes.
- Next add the zucchini, garlic powder, and potatoes along with the spices. Stir together and cook for 1 minute then pour in vegetable broth.
- Add red lentils. Lock the lid into place. Select Pressure Cook or Manual, and adjust the

pressure to High and the time to 20 minutes. After cooking, let the pressure release naturally
for 10 minutes, then quickly release any remaining pressure.
• Unlock the lid. Squeeze in the lemon juice and stir together. Garnish with fresh cilantro.

Nutrition:
• Calories 383, Total Fat 9. 3g, Saturated Fat 6. 5g, Cholesterol 0mg, Sodium 784mg, Total Carbohydrate 56. 6g, Dietary Fiber 19. 3g, Total Sugars 6. 5g, Protein 20. 9g

White Bean Spinach & Tomato Curry

• Preparation Time: 15 minutes | Cooking Time: 25 minutes | Servings: 2

Ingredients:
- 1 teaspoon vegetable oil
- 1 small onion, diced
- 1 zucchini, peeled and diced
- ½ teaspoon garlic, powder
- ½ teaspoon dried basil
- ¼ teaspoon salt
- ¼ teaspoon pepper
- 1/2 teaspoon crushed red pepper
- ½ cup spinach chopped
- 1 cup white beans, drained and rinsed
- ½ cup tomatoes
- 1 1/2 cups vegetable broth

Directions:

• Select the Sauté setting on the Instant Pot, add the vegetable oil, and heat for 1 minute. Add the onion and sauté for 2 minutes, then add the zucchini, garlic powder, tomatoes, and seasonings (salt, pepper, and basil) and continue to sauté for another 2 minutes.

• Add the spinach to the Instant Pot and cook until it starts to wilt. Pour vegetable broth and white beans.

• Select Pressure Cook or Manual, and adjust the

pressure to High and the time to 20 minutes. After cooking, let the pressure release naturally for 10 minutes, then quickly release any remaining pressure.

• Unlock the lid and Serve.

Nutrition:

• Calories 418, Total Fat 4. 2g, Saturated Fat 0. 9g, Cholesterol 0mg, Sodium 708mg, Total Carbohydrate 70. 6g, Dietary Fiber 18. 1g, Total Sugars 6. 9g, Protein 28. 3g

Spinach, Red Lentil and Bean Curry

Ingredients:
- ½ cup red lentils
- 1/8 cup tomato puree
- 1/4 container plain yogurt
- ½ teaspoon garam masala
- ¼ teaspoon turmeric powder
- ¼ teaspoon ground cumin
- ¼ tablespoons coconut oil
- 1 onion, chopped
- 1 teaspoon garlic powder
- ½ teaspoon ginger powder
- 1 cup fresh spinach, coarsely chopped
- 2 tomatoes, chopped
- 1 1/2 cups vegetable broth
- ½ teaspoon fresh cilantro, chopped
- 1 cup mixed beans

Directions:

• In a bowl, stir together the tomato puree and yogurt. Season with garam masala, turmeric powder, ground cumin, and. Stir until creamy.
 • Select the Sauté setting on the Instant Pot, add the coconut oil, Stir in chopped onions, garlic powder, and ginger powder; cook until onions begin to brown. Stir in spinach; cook until dark green and wilted. Gradually stir in yogurt mixture. Then mix in

the tomato puree and cilantro.
- Stir lentils and mixed beans into the mixture pour vegetable broth mix well. Select Pressure Cook or Manual, and adjust the pressure to High and the time to 20 minutes. After cooking, let the pressure release naturally for 10 minutes, then quickly release any remaining pressure.
- Unlock the lid.
- Serve and enjoy.

Nutrition:
- Calories346, Total Fat 3. 1g, Saturated Fat 1. 9g, Cholesterol 2mg, Sodium 519mg, Total Carbohydrate 62. 4g, Dietary Fiber 25. 2g, Total Sugars 9. 7g, Protein 21. 8g

Coconut-Apple-Ginger Beans

Preparation Time: 25 minutes | Cooking Time: 22min | Servings: 2

Ingredients:
- 1 tablespoon vegetable oil
- ¼ teaspoon paprika
- ¼ teaspoon cumin seed
- ¼ teaspoon turmeric powder
- 1 small onion, finely chopped
- ¼ teaspoon garlic powder
- 1/8 teaspoon ginger powder
- 1 large apple
- 1 cup pinto beans
- 1 cup of coconut milk
- ½ tablespoon fresh lime juice
- Kosher salt
- Freshly ground pepper

Directions:
- Select the Sauté setting on the Instant Pot, add the vegetable oil. Cook paprika, cumin seed, and turmeric powder, stirring, until fragrant, about 30 seconds. Add chopped onions, garlic powder, and ginger powder and cook, stirring, until softened, about 1 minute.
- Add apples and pinto beans and stir to coat. Stir in coconut milk and 2 cups of water. Select Pressure Cook or Manual, and adjust the pressure to High

and the time to 20 minutes. After cooking, let the pressure release naturally for 10 minutes, then quickly release any remaining pressure.
• Unlock the lid. Add lime juice and season with salt and pepper.

Nutrition:
• Calories 339, Total Fat 11. 2g, Saturated Fat 4. 5g, Cholesterol 0mg, Sodium 11mg, Total Carbohydrate 51. 3g, Dietary Fiber 11. 5g, Total Sugars 14. 9g, Protein 11. 6g

Lentil Chili

• Preparation Time: 05 minutes | Cooking Time: 23 minutes | Servings: 2

Ingredients:
- 1 tablespoon butter
- 1 onion, chopped
- ½ teaspoon garlic powder
- ½ cup dry lentils
- ½ cup dry buckwheat
- 2 cups vegetable broth
- 1 cup tomatoes, chopped
- 1 teaspoon chili powder
- 1 teaspoon cumin seed
- Salt and pepper to taste

Directions:

• Select the Sauté setting on the Instant Pot, add the butter, and heat for 1 minute. Add onions and garlic powder and sauté for 2 minutes. Stir in the lentils and buckwheat. Add the broth, tomatoes, chili powder, cumin seed, and salt and pepper to taste.

• Select Pressure Cook or Manual, and adjust the pressure to High and the time to 20 minutes. After cooking, let the pressure release naturally for 10 minutes, then quickly release any remaining pressure.

• Adjust the salt and pepper and serve.

Nutrition:

• Calories 453, Total Fat 9. 8g, Saturated Fat 4. 5g, Cholesterol 15mg, Sodium 829mg, Total Carbohydrate 70. 5g, Dietary Fiber 21. 8g, Total Sugars 6. 7g, Protein 24. 8g

Lemony Lentils with Spinach

• Preparation Time: 10 minutes | Cooking Time: 20 minutes | Servings: 2

Ingredients:
- 1 tablespoon coconut oil
- 1 small onion, diced
- ½ carrot, diced
- ½ cup broccoli
- 1 teaspoon garlic powder
- ½ teaspoon kosher salt
- Ground black pepper to taste
- ½ teaspoon crushed red pepper flakes, or to taste
- ½ cup green lentils
- ½ cup diced tomatoes
- 1 cup vegetable broth
- ½ cup spinach, chopped
- 1 lemon, zest, and juice

Directions:

• Select the Sauté setting on the Instant Pot, add coconut oil and stir onions and carrots, and broccoli in the hot oil until softened, about 2 minutes. Add garlic powder, kosher salt, black pepper, and red pepper flakes; cook and stir to coat for 1 minute.

• Stir lentils, tomatoes, and their juice, and vegetable broth into onion mixture. Lock the lid into place. Select Pressure Cook or Manual, and adjust the pressure to High and the time to 12 minutes. After cooking, let the pressure release naturally for 10 minutes, then quickly release any remaining pressure.

• Add spinach, lemon zest, and lemon juice; cook until spinach is wilted, about 5 minutes. Season with salt and black pepper.

Nutrition:

• Calories291, Total Fat 8. 3g, Saturated Fat 6. 2g, Cholesterol 0mg, Sodium 987mg, Total Carbohydrate 39. 8g, Dietary Fiber 17. 4g, Total Sugars 5. 8g, Protein 16. 5g

Garlic Lentil Curry

Preparation Time: 10 minutes | Cooking Time: 15min | Servings: 2

Ingredients:
- ¼ cup dry brown lentils
- 1/4 cup dry red lentils
- 2 cups of water
- 5 whole garlic cloves
- ¼ teaspoon salt
- ¼ teaspoon ground coriander
- ¼ teaspoon cayenne pepper, or to taste
- 1/8 teaspoon turmeric powder
- 1 tablespoon butter
- 1 small onion, sliced
- ½ teaspoon cumin seeds
- 1/8 cup soy milk

Directions:
• Soak brown and red lentils in ample cool water for 1 hour to overnight. Drain and rinse. • Select the Sauté setting on the Instant Pot, add butter and stir onions, and cook, stirring often,

until they turn golden brown. Stir in the cumin seeds, and cook until fragrant, about 1 minute. Pour in the water, then add garlic, salt, ground coriander, turmeric powder, and cayenne pepper.

- Add both lentils.
- Select Pressure Cook or Manual, and adjust the pressure to High and the time to 12 minutes. After cooking, let the pressure release naturally for 10 minutes, then quickly release any remaining pressure.
- Stir soy milk into the lentils.

Nutrition:
- Calories 171, Total Fat 6. 5g, Saturated Fat 3. 8g, Cholesterol 15mg, Sodium 700mg, Total Carbohydrate 20. 3g, Dietary Fiber 8. 8g, Total Sugars 2. 7g, Protein 7. 9g

Moroccan Black-Eyed Peas

• Preparation Time: 15 minutes | Cooking Time: 30 minutes | Servings: 2

Ingredients:
- ½ cup dried black-eyed peas (cowpeas)
- 1 small onion, chopped
- 1 cup tomato paste
- 1 tablespoon coconut oil
- 1/8 cup chopped fresh cilantro
- ½ teaspoon garlic powder
- ½ teaspoons salt
- ½ teaspoon cumin powder
- ½ teaspoon paprika
- 1 teaspoon ginger powder
- 2 cups of water

Directions:

• Place black-eyed peas into a large container and cover with several inches of cool water; let it stand for 8 hours to overnight. Drain and rinse peas.

• Combine black-eyed peas, onions, tomato paste, coconut oil, cilantro, garlic powder, salt, cumin, paprika, and ginger powder in an Instant Pot; pour 2 cups of water over the pea mixture.

• Select Pressure Cook or Manual, and adjust the pressure to High and the time to 12 minutes. After cooking, let the pressure release naturally for 10 minutes, then quickly release any remaining

pressure.
- Serve and enjoy.

Nutrition:
- Calories 233, Total Fat 8. 1g, Saturated Fat 6g, Cholesterol 0mg, Sodium 733mg, Total Carbohydrate 37. 5g, Dietary Fiber 8. 4g, Total Sugars 17. 7g, Protein 9. 3g

Black-Eyed Pea Chowder

• Preparation Time: 15 minutes | Cooking Time: 30 minutes | Servings: 2

Ingredients:
- ½ cup chopped leeks
- 1 tablespoon olive oil
- ½ cup chopped onions
- 1 cup chopped green bell pepper
- ½ cup black-eyed peas
- 1 cup diced tomatoes
- ½ cup of corn
- 1 cup vegetable broth
- ½ cup kale

Directions:

• Select the Sauté setting on the Instant Pot, add olive oil and onions in the Instant Pot, and cook until tender. Add the green bell pepper, chopped leek, black-eyed peas, tomatoes, corn, and kale. Mix well.

• Pour vegetable broth. Select Pressure Cook or Manual, and adjust the pressure to High and the time to 12 minutes. After cooking, let the pressure release naturally for 10 minutes, then quickly release any remaining pressure.

• Open lid. Serve and enjoy.

Nutrition:

• Calories 147, Total Fat 1. 4g, Saturated Fat 0. 1g, Cholesterol 0mg, Sodium 37mg, Total Carbohydrate

30. 9g, Dietary Fiber 6. 2g, Total Sugars 8. 7g, Protein 6. 8g

Baked Barbeque Beans

- Preparation Time: 15 minutes | Cooking Time: 40 minutes | Servings: 2

Ingredients:
- ½ cup dry navy beans
- 2 cups of water
- ¼ teaspoon salt
- 1 small onion, finely chopped
- ¼ red or green bell pepper, cored, seeded, and finely chopped
- ¼ cup barbecue sauce
- ½ teaspoon mustard
- ¼ cup lemon juice
- ½ cup honey
- Enough water

Directions:

- Add navy beans, water, and salt into Instant Pot. Cook on Manual (High Pressure) for 25 minutes. Allow the pressure to naturally release.
- Remove the lid and pour beans into a colander/strainer. Rinse with cold water. Set aside.
- Set Instant Pot to Sauté setting. Add bell pepper and onions and cook until tender. Turn IP off. Add barbecue sauce, mustard, lemon juice to the Instant pot and stir well to combine. Add honey, water, and beans and stir to combine.
- Secure IP lid, close steam valve, and cook on Manual (High pressure) for 15 minutes. Allow the

pressure to naturally release.
• Carefully open the lid, and gently stir the mixture to combine. Enjoy!

Nutrition:
• Calories 510, Total Fat 1. 4g, Saturated Fat 0. 3g, Cholesterol 0mg, Sodium 661mg, Total Carbohydrate 118. 1g, Dietary Fiber 14. 2g, Total Sugars 82. 7g, Protein 12. 9g

Black Beans with Mint

• Preparation Time: 15 minutes | Cooking Time: 40 minutes | Servings: 2

Ingredients:
- ½ cup dried black beans
- 1 tablespoon coconut oil
- ½ cup chopped onions
- ½ cup chopped red bell pepper
- ¼ medium jalapeno pepper, seeded and finely chopped
- 1 teaspoon garlic powder
- ½ teaspoons salt
- ½ teaspoon cumin seed
- ¼ teaspoon coriander powder
- 1/8 teaspoon dried basil
- 1 bay leaves
- 2 cups vegetable stock
- ½ cup halved cherry tomatoes
- ½ cup chopped mint leaves

Directions:
• Set an Instant Pot to Sauté. Allow to heat for 3 minutes. Add coconut oil, onions, red bell peppers, jalapeno pepper, garlic powder, salt, cumin seed, coriander powder, and basil. Cook stirring often, about 5 minutes.

• Add bay leaves, stock, and black beans. Stir to blend. Cover Instant Pot, and fasten the lid. Lock and seal steam valve. Set to High Pressure for 30 minutes.

• When the cooking time has ended, allow Instant Pot to naturally release pressure for 20 minutes. Uncover and turn off Instant Pot.
• To serve, spoon beans and cooking liquid into bowls and top evenly with cherry tomatoes and mint leaves.

Nutrition:
• Calories 277, Total Fat 8. 1g, Saturated Fat 6. 1g, Cholesterol 0mg, Sodium 646mg, Total Carbohydrate 41. 3g, Dietary Fiber 11. 3g, Total Sugars 6g, Protein 13g

Curried Pinto Beans

• Preparation Time: 15 minutes | Cooking Time: 30 minutes | Servings: 2

Ingredients:
- ¼ teaspoon of sea salt
- ½ tablespoon garlic powder
- ½ cup onion, chopped
- ½ teaspoon dried rosemary
- 1 cup dried pinto beans
- 2 cups vegetable broth

Directions:

• Place all ingredients into the Instant Pot. Add 2 cups of vegetable broth. Stir to mix. • Cover with the lid and ensure the vent is in the —Sealing‖ position. Pressure Cook on High for

30 minutes. Allow the steam pressure to release naturally for 20 minutes.
• Serve and enjoy.

Nutrition:

• Calories 393, Total Fat 2. 7g, Saturated Fat 0. 6g, Cholesterol 0mg, Sodium 1011mg, Total Carbohydrate 65. 7g, Dietary Fiber 15. 9g, Total Sugars 4. 5g, Protein 26. 2g

Pinto Beans Curry

• Preparation Time: 15 minutes | Cooking Time: 60 minutes | Servings: 2

Ingredients:
- ½ tablespoon butter
- 1 red onion
- ½ teaspoon garlic powder
- 1 1/2 cup dry pinto beans
- 1 bay leaf
- Freshly cracked pepper
- 2 cups reduced-sodium vegetable broth
- ½ cup diced tomatoes

Directions:

• Add butter, onion, garlic powder, pinto beans, bay leaves, pepper, and broth to the pot, stir briefly to combine, then place the lid on the Instant Pot. Close the steam valve, press the Manual button, select High pressure, then press the + button to increase the time to 35 minutes.

• Allow the pinto beans to cook through the 35-minute cycle, then let the pressure release naturally (you'll know the pressure has been released when the silver float valve has fallen back down and is no longer flush with the top of the lid).

• Once the pressure has been released, open the steam valve, and then remove the lid. Discard the bay leaf. Add the diced tomatoes with all their juices, then stir to combine.

• Press the Cancel button to Cancel the "keep warm" function, then press the Sauté button and use the Adjust button to select the "Normal" heat level. Let the mixture simmer, stirring often, until the beans are very tender and the liquid has thickened.

• Serve and enjoy.

Nutrition:

• Calories 409, Total Fat 4. 3g, Saturated Fat 2. 1g, Cholesterol 8mg, Sodium 567mg, Total Carbohydrate 71g, Dietary Fiber 17. 9g, Total Sugars 7. 7g, Protein 21. 9g

Tempeh White Bean Gravy

• Preparation Time: 05 minutes | Cooking Time: 20 minutes | Servings: 2

Ingredients:
- ½ cup cups vegetable broth
- ¼ cup of soy sauce
- ¼ cup of coconut oil
- 1 teaspoon garlic powder
- ½ cup chopped onion
- 1 cup chopped tempeh
- 1/8 teaspoon dried basil
- 1/8 teaspoon dried parsley
- 1/8 teaspoon ground black pepper
- 1 cup white beans, drained and rinsed
- Enough water

Directions:
- Add vegetable broth, soy sauce, coconut oil, garlic powder, onion, tempeh, basil, parsley, black pepper, and white beans to the Instant Pot. Pour the remaining ¼ cup water over everything.
- Choose the soup function for 20 minutes.
- Once done, remove the lid.
- Serve and enjoy.

Nutrition:
- Calories 376, Total Fat 29. 4g, Saturated Fat 23. 6g, Cholesterol 0mg, Sodium 2233mg, Total Carbohydrate 22. 4g, Dietary Fiber 4. 9g, Total Sugars 4. 2g, Protein 9. 2g

Three-Bean Chili

- Preparation Time: 10 minutes | Cooking Time: 30 minutes | Servings: 2 Ingredients:
- ¼ cup dried pinto beans soaked 8 hours or overnight
- ¼ cup dried kidney beans soaked 8 hours or overnight
- ¼ cup dried black beans soaked 8 hours or overnight
- ½ tablespoon olive oil
- 1 small onion chopped
- 1 teaspoon salt
- ½ tablespoon tomato paste
- ½ teaspoon garlic powder
- 1 teaspoon paprika
- 1 teaspoon cumin powder
- ½ teaspoon coriander powder
- ½ cup crushed tomatoes 1 can
- 2 cups of water
- Chopped fresh cilantro

Directions:

- Drain and rinse beans. Press Sauté; to the Instant Pot. Cook for 3 to 4 minutes. Remove to a bowl.
- Heat olive oil in Instant Pot. Add onion, cook, and stir for 3 minutes or until softened. Add salt, tomato paste, garlic powder, paprika, cumin powder, and coriander powder; cook and stir for 1 minute. Stir in tomatoes, water, beans; mix well.

• Secure lid and move pressure release valve to sealing position. Press Manual or Pressure Cook; cook at High pressure 20 minutes.
• When cooking is complete, use Natural-release for 10 minutes, then release remaining pressure. Garnish with cilantro.

Nutrition:
• Calories 120, Total Fat 4. 1g, Saturated Fat 0. 6g, Cholesterol 0mg, Sodium 1221mg, Total Carbohydrate 22. 4g, Dietary Fiber 10g, Total Sugars 2. 8g, Protein 7. 4g

Broccoli and Black Bean Chili

• Preparation Time: 15 minutes | Cooking Time: 15 minutes | Servings: 2

Ingredients:
- ½ tablespoon coconut oil
- 1 cup broccoli
- 1 cup chopped red onions
- ½ tablespoon paprika
- 1/2 teaspoon salt
- ¼ cup tomatoes
- 1 cup black beans drained, rinsed
- ¼ chopped green chills
- ½ cup of water

Directions:

• In the Instant Pot, select Sauté; adjust to normal. Heat coconut oil in Instant Pot. Add broccoli, onions, paprika, and salt; cook 8 to 10 minutes, stirring occasionally, until thoroughly cooked. Select Cancel.

• Stir in tomatoes, black beans, chills, and water. Secure lid set pressure valve to Sealing. Select Manual, cook on High pressure 5 minutes. Select Cancel. Keep the pressure valve in the Sealing position to release pressure naturally.

Nutrition:

• Calories 408, Total Fat 5. 3g, Saturated Fat 3. 4g, Cholesterol 0mg, Sodium 607mg, Total Carbohydrate 70. 7g, Dietary Fiber 18. 1g, Total Sugars 6g, Protein 23. 3g

Potato and Chickpea Curry

• Preparation Time: 05 minutes | Cooking Time: 10 minutes | Servings: 2

Ingredients:
- ½ tablespoon coconut oil
- 1 small onion chopped
- 2 teaspoons paprika
- ½ teaspoon garlic powder
- ¼ teaspoon salt
- ¼ teaspoon chipotle chili powder
- ¼ teaspoon ground cumin
- 1 cup vegetable broth
- 1 cup chickpea rinsed and drained
- ¼ cup potatoes peeled and cut into 1/2-inch pieces
- ½ cup diced tomatoes

Directions:

• Press Sauté, heat coconut oil in Instant Pot. Add chopped onions; cook 3 minutes or until softened. Add paprika, garlic powder, salt, chipotle chili powder, and ground cumin; cook and stir for 1 minute. Stir in broth, scraping up browned bits from the bottom of Instant Pot. Add chickpea, potatoes, and diced tomatoes; mix well.

• Secure lid and move pressure release valve to the Sealing position. Press Manual or Pressure Cook; cook at High Pressure for 4 minutes.

• When cooking is complete, press Cancel and use Quick-release.

• Press Sauté; cook and stir for 3 to 5 minutes or until thickened to desired consistency. Serve with desired toppings.

Nutrition:
• Calories 575, Total Fat 11. 3g, Saturated Fat 3. 8g, Cholesterol 0mg, Sodium 679mg, Total Carbohydrate 96. 2g, Dietary Fiber 25. 1g, Total Sugars 13. 8g, Protein 26. 7g

Vegetarian Chili

- Preparation Time: 15 minutes | Cooking Time: 20 minutes | Servings: 2 Ingredients:

  - 1 tablespoon avocado oil
  - ½ teaspoon garlic powder
  - 1 cup chopped onion
  - ½ cup chopped carrots
  - ¼ cup chopped green bell pepper
  - ¼ cup chopped red bell pepper
  - 1 tablespoon chili powder
  - ½ cup chopped fresh mushrooms
  - ½ cup whole peeled tomatoes with liquid, chopped
  - ¼ cup black beans
  - ¼ cup kidney beans
  - ¼ cup pinto beans
  - ¼ cup whole kernel corn
  - ½ tablespoon cumin seed
  - 1/2 tablespoons dried basil
  - 1/2 tablespoon garlic minced

Directions:

- Select the Sauté setting on the Instant Pot, add avocado oil, cook and stir the garlic minced, onions, and carrots in the Instant Pot until tender. Mix in the green bell pepper, red bell pepper, and chili powder. Season with chili powder. Continue cooking for 2 minutes, or until the peppers are tender.
- Mix the mushrooms into the Instant pot. Stir in the tomatoes with liquid, black beans, kidney

beans, pinto beans, and corn. Season with cumin seed, basil, and garlic powder.

• Select Pressure Cook or Manual, and adjust the pressure to High and the time to 12 minutes. After cooking, let the pressure release naturally for 10 minutes, then quickly release any remaining pressure.

Nutrition:

• Calories 348, Total Fat 3. 3g, Saturated Fat 0. 6g, Cholesterol 0mg, Sodium 77mg, Total Carbohydrate 65g, Dietary Fiber 16. 5g, Total Sugars 9. 5g, Protein 19. 1g

Coconut Curry Chili

• Preparation Time: 15 minutes | Cooking Time: 30 minutes | Servings: 2

Ingredients:
- 1 cup tomatoes
- 2 cups of water
- 1 tablespoon minced garlic
- ½ cup garbanzo beans
- ½ cup red kidney beans
- 1/2 cup chopped zucchini
- ¼ cup mango
- 1 1/2 tablespoons curry powder
- 1cup onions, chopped
- Salt and ground black pepper to taste
- ½ cup of coconut milk

Directions:

• In the Instant Pot, add all ingredients like tomatoes, water, garlic, garbanzo beans, kidney beans, zucchini, mango, curry powder, onions, salt, and black pepper.
• Select Pressure Cook or Manual, and adjust the pressure to High and the time to 12 minutes. After cooking, let the pressure release naturally for 10 minutes, then quickly release any remaining pressure.
• Stir coconut milk.
• Serve.

Nutrition:

• Calories 548, Total Fat 18. 6g, Saturated Fat 13. 2g, Cholesterol 0mg, Sodium 46mg, Total Carbohydrate 78g, Dietary Fiber 21. 1g, Total Sugars 16. 6g, Protein 24g

Spicy Butternut Squash Chili

- Preparation Time: 15 minutes | Cooking Time: 30 minutes | Servings: 2

Ingredients:
- ½ teaspoon crushed red pepper flakes, or to taste
- 1 teaspoon garlic powder
- ½ large onion, diced
- 1 green bell pepper, chopped
- 1 red bell pepper, chopped
- ½ cup kidney beans
- ½ cup black beans
- ½ cup pinto beans,
- 1 cup tomato paste
- 2 tomatoes, diced
- ½ cup butter squash diced
- ½ cup green peas
- ½ teaspoons chili powder
- 1 teaspoon cumin
- Salt and pepper

Directions:

- In the Instant Pot, combine red pepper flakes, garlic powder, onion, kidney beans, black beans, pinto beans, tomato paste, diced tomatoes, and butter squash.
- Add the green and red bell pepper and water and cook for 5 minutes. Season with chili powder,

cumin, and salt.
- Stir the green peas, salt, and pepper into the Instant pot. Select Pressure Cook or Manual, and adjust the pressure to High and the time to 12 minutes. After cooking, let the pressure release naturally for 10 minutes, then quickly release any remaining pressure.
- Serve and enjoy.

Nutrition:
- Calories 620, Total Fat 2. 9g, Saturated Fat 0. 6g, Cholesterol 0mg, Sodium 37mg, Total Carbohydrate 117. 2g, Dietary Fiber 29. 3g, Total Sugars 16. 1g, Protein 37g

Creamy White Beans and Chickpeas Chili

• Preparation Time: 05 minutes | Cooking Time: 35 minutes | Servings: 2

Ingredients:
- 1 teaspoon coconut oil
- 1 onion finely diced
- ½ teaspoon garlic powder
- 2 cups vegetable broth
- ½ cup chickpeas
- ½ cup navy beans
- ½ tablespoon chili powder
- ½ cumin powder
- ½ teaspoon kosher salt
- ¼ teaspoon black pepper
- 1/2 cup butter
- 3 tablespoon coconut flour
- 1 cup coconut milk warmed
- ¼ cup coconut cream
- ½ tablespoon lime juice

Directions:
• Add coconut oil to the Instant Pot. Using the display panel select the Sauté function.
• When oil gets hot, add onion to the pot and sauté until soft, 3-4 minutes. Add garlic powder

and cook for 1-2 minutes more.

• Add broth to the pot and deglaze by using a wooden spoon to scrape the brown bits from the bottom of the pot.

• Add chickpeas, beans, chili and cumin powder, salt, and pepper, and stir to combine. • Turn the pot off by selecting Cancel, then secure the lid, making sure the vent is closed. • Using the display panel select the Manual or Pressure Cook function. Use the + /- keys and

program the Instant Pot for 15 minutes.

• When the time is up, let the pressure naturally release for 10 minutes, then quickly release the remaining pressure.

• In a medium bowl, melt butter, then whisk in flour until well combined. Stir into the pot and simmer 3-5 minutes until thickened, returning to Sauté mode as needed.

• Stir in coconut milk, coconut cream, and lime juice. Adjust seasonings.

Nutrition:

• Calories 1086, Total Fat 71. 3g, Saturated Fat 47. 6g, Cholesterol 122mg, Sodium 1764mg, Total Carbohydrate 86. 3g, Dietary Fiber 32. 3g, Total Sugars 14. 5g, Protein 32. 1g

Potato Chili

• Preparation Time: 10 minutes | Cooking Time: 25 minutes | Servings: 2

Ingredients:
- ½ teaspoon olive oil
- ½ cup onion chopped
- ½ teaspoon garlic powder
- ½ teaspoon chili powder
- ½ teaspoon ground cumin
- 1 cup diced tomatoes
- ½ cup black beans rinsed and drained
- 1 medium red bell pepper seeded and diced
- 1 medium potato peeled and diced
- 1 teaspoon kosher salt
- ¼ cup frozen corn kernels

Directions:

• Select Sauté and add the olive oil to the Instant Pot. Add the onions and garlic powder. Sauté for 2 minutes, or until the garlic powder is fragrant and the onion is soft and translucent.

• Add the chili powder and ground cumin, followed by the tomatoes, black beans, red bell pepper, potato, corn, and salt. Stir well.

• Cover, lock the lid and flip the steam release handle to the Sealing position. Select Pressure Cook High and set the cooking time for 15 minutes. When the cooking time is complete, allow the pressure to release naturally for about 20 minutes.

• Remove the lid and ladle the chili into serving bowls. Serve hot.

Nutrition:
• Calories 207, Total Fat 2. 1g, Saturated Fat 0. 3g, Cholesterol 0mg, Sodium 1207mg, Total Carbohydrate 41. 4g, Dietary Fiber 8. 8g, Total Sugars 7. 7g, Protein 8. 2g

Beans Baby Potato Curry

• Preparation Time: 10 minutes | Cooking Time: 30 minutes | Servings: 2

Ingredients:
- 1 small onion, chopped
- ½ teaspoon garlic, chopped finely
- 1 cup baby potatoes
- ½ tablespoon curry powder
- 2 cups of water
- ½ cup pinto beans
- ½ cup milk
- ½ tablespoon honey
- Salt & pepper to taste
- ½ teaspoon chili pepper flakes
- 1 tablespoon arrowroot powder

Directions:

• Set your Instant Pot to Sauté. Once hot, add a few drops of water and cook the onions until translucent, then add the garlic and cook for one minute longer. Press the Keep Warm/Cancel button.

• Add everything to the Instant Pot except the arrowroot powder.

• Set the Instant Pot to 20 minutes on Manual High pressure and allow the pressure to release naturally after this time.

• Press Keep Warm/Cancel, remove the lid, and press Sauté. Put the arrowroot into a small bowl or cup and mix into it a few tablespoons of water to make a thickness but pour slurry. Pour it into the Instant Pot stirring as you go.

• Add salt and pepper to taste then cook for about 5 minutes until they are tender and the gravy has thickened.

• Serve immediately.

Nutrition:

• Calories342, Total Fat 2. 3g, Saturated Fat 1g, Cholesterol 5mg, Sodium 58mg, Total Carbohydrate 67. 2g, Dietary Fiber 12. 1g, Total Sugars 10g, Protein 14. 2g

Butter Tofu with Soy Bean and Chickpeas

• Preparation Time: 10 minutes | Cooking Time: 30 minutes | Servings: 2

Ingredients:
- 2 large ripe tomatoes
- ½ teaspoon garlic powder
- ½ teaspoon ginger powder
- ½ tablespoon hot green chili
- 1 cup of water
- ¼ teaspoon garam masala
- 1/8 teaspoon paprika
- ¼ teaspoon salt
- ¼ cup of soybeans
- ½ cup chickpeas
- ½ teaspoon honey
- ½ cup coconut cream
- Cilantro for garnish

Directions:
• Blend the tomatoes, garlic powder, ginger powder, hot green chili with water until smooth. • Add pureed tomato mixture to the Instant Pot. Add soybeans, chickpeas, spices, and salt.

Close the lid and cook on Manual for 8 to 10 minutes. Quick-release after 10 minutes. • Start the Instant Pot on Sauté. Add the coconut cream,

Garam masala, honey, and mix in.
 Bring to a boil, taste, and adjust salt. Add more paprika and salt if needed.
 • Serve with cilantro garnishing

Nutrition:
 • Calories 242, Total Fat 1. 3g, Saturated Fat 1. 5g, Cholesterol 5mg, Sodium 38mg, Total Carbohydrate 47. 2g, Dietary Fiber 10. 1g, Total Sugars 10g, Protein 14. 2g.

Black Eyed Peas Curry with Jaggery

• Preparation Time: 10 minutes | Cooking Time: 30 minutes | Servings: 2

Ingredients:
- ¼ cup dried black-eyed peas, soaked in water for about 1-2 hours
- 2 cups of water
- 1 dried curry leaves
- 1/8 teaspoon mustard seeds
- ½ teaspoon garlic powder
- 1/2 small onion, finely chopped
- 2 tablespoons tomato paste
- ½ teaspoon ground cumin
- 1 teaspoon ground coriander
- ¼ teaspoon ground turmeric
- 1 tablespoon jaggery
- 1 tablespoon fresh lemon juice
- Chili powder, to taste (optional
- 1 tablespoon avocado oil
- Salt
- Fresh cilantro, finely chopped

Directions:
- Select the Sauté button into the Instant Pot and add avocado oil.
- Once the oil is hot, add the mustard seeds and curry leaves. Fry for a few seconds until

fragrant.
- Add the onions and garlic powder. Sauté until fragrant and the onions start to become translucent. Be sure not to burn either. If you see this happening add more oil or turn down the sauté heat.
- Quickly add the tomato paste, ground cumin, and ground coriander. Combine and cook for a minute mixing frequently.
- Drain the soaked black-eyed peas and add them into the Instant Pot.
- Mix in the water, turmeric powder, chili powder, jaggery, fresh lemon juice, and salt. • Close the Instant Pot lid, select the Pressure Cook button to cook on High. Set the timer for about 13-15 minutes.
- When the time is up, allow the pressure to release naturally.
- Once the pressure has been released, remove the lid, and press the Sauté (normally Low) button again on the Instant Pot. The black-eyed peas should be fully cooked. • Simmer for a few more minutes until the curry becomes thick.
- Add salt to taste. Also, feel free to adjust the amount of lemon juice and jaggery as needed. • Turn the Instant Pot off. Add freshly chopped cilantro and serve hot.

Nutrition:
- Calories79, Total Fat 0. 9g, Saturated Fat 0. 2g, Cholesterol 0mg, Sodium 75mg, Total Carbohydrate

18g, Dietary Fiber 4. 7g, Total Sugars 8. 2g, Protein 4g

Jackfruit with Beans Curry

• Preparation Time: 10 minutes | Cooking Time: 20 minutes | Servings: 2

Ingredients:
- ½ tablespoon coconut oil
- ½ tablespoon curry powder
- ¼ teaspoon paprika
- ½ teaspoon cumin seeds
- ¼ teaspoon turmeric powder
- 1 sprigs fresh rosemary
- ½ cup onion, finely chopped
- 1 teaspoon garlic powder
- 1 teaspoon ginger powder
- 1 celery, chopped
- 1 cup jackfruit, drained and rinsed
- ½ cup pinto beans
- ½ medium zucchini, diced
- ½ cup full-fat milk
- 1 cups vegetable broth
- 1/4 cup parsley leaves, chopped
- Salt, to taste

Directions:
• Plug your Instant Pot and press the Sauté mode button. Add coconut oil, once heated add dry spices, curry powder, paprika, cumin seeds, turmeric powder, rosemary, and cook for a minute stirring constantly.

• Add onions, garlic powder, ginger powder, and celery, and cook for 2 minutes or until onions are soft. Add jackfruit, pinto beans, zucchini and stir to coat.

- Add salt, milk, and vegetable broth.
- Close the Instant Pot lid and press Manual mode for 10 minutes. When finished, allow Instant Pot to natural release for 10 minutes. Carefully release the knob to release the remaining pressure. Remove lid, stir in parsley leaves, and check seasonings.
- Serve.

Nutrition:
- Calories320, Total Fat 5. 5g, Saturated Fat 3. 5g, Cholesterol 1mg, Sodium 582mg, Total Carbohydrate 50. 7g, Dietary Fiber 17. 6g, Total Sugars 7g, Protein 17. 5g

Smoky, Black Beans Chickpeas, and Corn

• Preparation Time: 05 minutes | Cooking Time: 10 minutes | Servings: 2

Ingredients:
- 2 teaspoons ground cumin
- ½ cup onion, chopped
- 1 teaspoon garlic powder
- ¼ teaspoon salt
- 1 cup black beans
- ½ cup chickpea
- ½ cup dried corn
- 2 cups vegetable broth or water
- Chopped fresh cilantro to serve
- Lime juice to serve

Directions:
• Place all ingredients into the Instant Pot. Add 2 cups of broth or water. Stir to mix. Cover with the lid and ensure the vent is in the —Sealing‖ position. Pressure Cook on High for 5 minutes. Allow the steam pressure to release naturally for 5 minutes, then release any remaining pressure manually.
• Garnish with fresh cilantro and a squeeze of lime juice.

Nutrition:
• Calories 616, Total Fat 6. 8g, Saturated Fat 1. 2g, Cholesterol 0mg, Sodium 1087mg, Total

Carbohydrate 105. 8g, Dietary Fiber 25. 9g, Total Sugars 11. 4g, Protein 37. 9g

Coconut Salad

Preparation Time: 10 minutes | Cooking Time: 0 minutes | Servings: 6

Ingredients:
- 2 cups coconut flesh, unsweetened and shredded
- ½ cup walnuts, chopped
- 1 cup blackberries
- 1 tablespoon stevia
- 1 tablespoon coconut oil, melted

Directions:
- In a bowl, combine the coconut with the walnuts and the other ingredients, toss and serve. Nutrition:
- Calories 250, Fat 23.8, Fiber 5.8, Carbs 8.9, Protein 4.5

Avocado and Rhubarb Salad

Preparation Time: 10 minutes | Cooking Time: 0 minutes | Servings: 4

Ingredients:
- 1 tablespoon stevia
- 1 cup rhubarb, sliced and boiled
- 2 avocados, peeled, pitted, and sliced
- 1 teaspoon vanilla extract
- Juice of 1 lime

Directions:
- In a bowl, combine the rhubarb with the avocado and the other ingredients, toss and serve. Nutrition:
- Calories 140, Fat 2, Fiber 2, Carbs 4, Protein 4

Vegetable Mushroom Side Dish

• Preparation Time: 15-30 minutes | Cooking Time: 85 minutes | Servings: 4

Ingredients:
- 2 tbsp plant butter
- 1 large onion, diced
- 1 cup celery, diced
- ½ cup carrots, diced
- ½ tsp dried marjoram
- 1 tsp dried basil
- 2 cups chopped cremini mushrooms
- 1 cup vegetable broth
- ¼ cup chopped fresh parsley
- 1 medium whole-grain bread loaf, cubed

Directions:

• Melt the butter in a large skillet and sauté the onion, celery, mushrooms, and carrots until softened, 5 minutes.
• Mix in the marjoram, basil, and season with salt and black pepper.
• Pour in the vegetable broth and mix in the parsley and bread. Cook until the broth reduces by half, 10 minutes.
• Pour the mixture into a baking dish and cover with foil. Bake in the oven at 375 F for 30 minutes.
• Uncover and bake further for 30 minutes or until golden brown on top and the liquid absorbs.

• Remove the dish from the oven and serve the stuffing.

Nutrition:
• Calories 575 kcal Fats 60. 9g Carbs 10. 3g Protein 3. 3g

Asian Dumplings

• Preparation Time: 32 minutes | Cooking Time: 15-120 minutes | Servings: 12 Dumplings

Ingredients:
- 1 1/12 Tablespoons Sesame Oil
- 3 Cloves Garlic, minced
- 1 Tablespoon Fresh Ginger, minced
- 1 Cup Mushrooms, minced
- 1/2 cup Tamari Sauce, Soy Sauce, or Coconut Aminos(for soy-free)
- 1 Teaspoon Sriracha
- 1 Tablespoon Rice Vinegar
- 1 Tablespoon Sesame Seeds
- 12 Vegan Dumpling Wrappers
- 1 1/2 Cups Water(for steaming

Directions:
- On saute mode, heat the sesame oil. When hot, add garlic and ginger. Cook for 1 minute. • Add mushrooms and saute until juices are released from mushrooms.
- Add tamari, soy sauce, or coconut aminos, sriracha, rice vinegar, and sesame seeds. Saute

until all liquid is cooked out.
- Prepare a small bowl of water. Lay a wrapper and spread water around the edge with fingers. • Fill each dumpling with 1

tablespoon of filling in the middle of the wrapper and press edges

together to seal. Place each dumpling onto the vegetable steamer that is lightly coated with oil.
• After all wrappers are made, remove the liner from the instant pot and add water.
• Place the vegetable steamer filled with dumplings into the instant pot. Cover with lid and seal. Select the steam option and set it to 7 minutes.
• When done, open the steam release valve manually.
• Serve immediately with tamari sauce, soy sauce, coconut aminos, or sriracha for dipping.
• Enjoy!

Nutrition:
• Calories: 140 Cal Fat: 0.9 g Carbs: 27.1 g Protein: 6.3 g Fiber: 6.2 g

Lentil and Wild Rice Soup

• Preparation Time: 10 minutes | Cooking Time: 40 minutes | Servings: 4

- 1/2 cup cooked mixed beans
- 12 ounces cooked lentils
- 2 stalks of celery, sliced
- 1 1/2 cup mixed wild rice, cooked
- 1 large sweet potato, peeled, chopped
- 1/2 medium butternut, peeled, chopped
- 4 medium carrots, peeled, sliced
- 1 medium onion, peeled, diced
- 10 cherry tomatoes
- 1/2 red chili, deseeded, diced
- 1 ½ teaspoon minced garlic
- 1/2 teaspoon salt
- 2 teaspoons mixed dried herbs
- 1 teaspoon coconut oil
- 2 cups vegetable broth

Directions:

• Take a large pot, place it over medium-high heat, add oil and when it melts, add onion and cook for 5 minutes.

• Stir in garlic and chili, cook for 3 minutes, then add remaining vegetables, pour in the broth, stir and bring the mixture to a boil.

• Switch heat to medium-low heat, cook the soup for 20 minutes, then stir in remaining ingredients and continue cooking for 10 minutes until soup has

reached the desired thickness.
- Serve straight away.

Nutrition:
- Calories: 331 Cal Fat: 2 g Carbs: 54 g Protein: 13 g Fiber: 12 g

Garlic and White Bean Soup

• Preparation Time: 10 minutes | Cooking Time: 10 minutes | Servings: 4

Ingredients:
• 45 ounces cooked cannellini beans
• 1/4 teaspoon dried thyme
• 2 teaspoons minced garlic
• 1/8 teaspoon crushed red pepper
• 1/2 teaspoon dried rosemary
• 1/8 teaspoon ground black pepper
• 2 tablespoons olive oil
• 4 cups vegetable broth

Directions:
• Place one-third of white beans in a food processor, then pour in 2 cups of broth and pulse for

2 minutes until smooth.

• Place a pot over medium heat, add oil and when hot, add garlic and cook for 1 minute until fragrant. Add pureed beans into the pan along with remaining beans, sprinkle with spices and herbs, pour in the broth, stir until combined, and bring the mixture to boil over mediumhigh heat. Switch heat to medium-low level, simmer the beans for 15 minutes, and then mash them with a fork. Taste the soup to adjust seasoning and then serve.

Nutrition:
• Calories: 222 Cal Fat: 7 g Carbs: 13 g Protein:

11. 2 g Fiber: 9. 1 g

Vegetarian Irish Stew

Preparation Time: 5 minutes | Cooking Time: 38 minutes | Servings: 6

Ingredients:

- 1 cup textured vegetable protein, chunks
- ½ cup split red lentils
- 2 medium onions, peeled, sliced
- 1 cup sliced parsnip
- 2 cups sliced mushrooms
- 1 cup diced celery,
- 1/4 cup flour
- 4 cups vegetable stock
- 1 cup rutabaga
- 1 bay leaf
- ½ cup fresh parsley
- 1 teaspoon sugar
- ¼ teaspoon ground black pepper
- 1/4 cup soy sauce
- ¼ teaspoon thyme
- 2 teaspoons marmite
- ¼ teaspoon rosemary
- 2/3 teaspoon salt
- ¼ teaspoon marjoram

Directions:

• Take a large soup pot, place it over medium heat, add oil and when it gets hot, add onions and cook for 5 minutes until softened.

• Then switch heat to the low level, sprinkle with

flour, stir well, add remaining ingredients, stir until combined, and simmer for 30 minutes until vegetables have cooked.

• When done, season the stew with salt and black pepper and then serve.

Nutrition:

• Calories: 117.4 Cal Fat: 4 g Carbs: 22.8 g Protein: 6.5 g Fiber: 7.3 g

White Bean and Cabbage Stew

Preparation Time: 5 minutes | Cooking Time: 8 hours | Servings: 4

- 3 cups cooked great northern beans
- 1.5 pounds potatoes, peeled, cut into large dice
- 1 large white onion, peeled, chopped
- ½ head of cabbage, chopped
- 3 ribs celery, chopped
- 4 medium carrots, peeled, sliced
- 14.5 ounces diced tomatoes
- 1/3 cup pearled barley
- 1 teaspoon minced garlic
- ½ teaspoon ground black pepper
- 1 bay leaf
- 1 teaspoon dried thyme
- ½ teaspoon crushed rosemary
- 1 teaspoon salt
- ½ teaspoon caraway seeds
- 1 tablespoon chopped parsley
- 8 cups vegetable broth

Directions:

• Switch on the slow cooker, then add all the ingredients except for salt, parsley, tomatoes, and beans and stir until mixed.
• Shut the slow cooker with a lid, and cook for 7 hours at a low heat setting until cooked.
• Then stir in remaining ingredients, stir until

combined, and continue cooking for 1 hour.
  • Serve straight away

Nutrition:
  • Calories: 150 Cal Fat: 0.7 g Carbs: 27 g Protein:
7 g Fiber: 9.4 g

Spinach and Cannellini Bean Stew

• Preparation Time: 10 minutes | Cooking Time: 15 minutes | Servings: 6

Ingredients:
- 28 ounces cooked cannellini beans
- 24 ounces tomato passata
- 17 ounces spinach chopped
- ¼ teaspoon ground black pepper
- 2/3 teaspoon salt
- 1 ¼ teaspoon curry powder
- 1 cup cashew butter
- ¼ teaspoon cardamom
- 2 tablespoons olive oil
- 1 teaspoon salt
- ¼ cup cashews
- 2 tablespoons chopped basil
- 2 tablespoons chopped parsley

Directions:

• Take a large saucepan, place it over medium heat, add 1 tablespoon oil and when hot, add spinach and cook for 3 minutes until fried.
• Then stir in butter and tomato passata until well mixed, bring the mixture to a near boil, add beans, and season with ¼ teaspoon curry powder, black pepper, and salt.
• Take a small saucepan, place it over medium heat, add remaining oil, stir in cashew, stir in salt

and curry powder and cook for 4 minutes until roasted, set aside until required.

• Transfer cooked stew into a bowl, top with roasted cashews, basil, and parsley, and then serve.

Nutrition:

• Calories: 242 Cal Fat: 10.2 g Carbs: 31 g Protein: 11 g Fiber: 8.5 g

Cabbage Stew

- Preparation Time: 10 minutes | Cooking Time: 50 minutes | Servings: 6

Ingredients:
- 12 ounces cooked Cannellini beans
- 8 ounces smoked tofu, firm, sliced
- 1 medium cabbage, chopped
- 1 large white onion, peeled, julienned
- 2 ½ teaspoon minced garlic
- 1 tablespoon sweet paprika
- 5 tablespoons tomato paste
- 3 teaspoons smoked paprika
- 1/3 teaspoon ground black pepper
- 2 teaspoons dried thyme
- 2/3 teaspoon salt
- ½ tsp ground coriander
- 3 bay leaves
- 4 tablespoons olive oil
- 1 cup vegetable broth

Directions:

- Take a large saucepan, place it over medium heat, add 3 tablespoons oil and when hot, add onion and garlic and cook for 3 minutes or until saute.
- Add cabbage, pour in water, simmer for 10 minutes or until softened, then stir in all the spices and continue cooking for 30 minutes.
- Add beans and tomato paste, pour in water, stir until mixed and cook for 15 minutes until

thoroughly cooked.
- Take a separate skillet pan, add 1 tablespoon oil and when hot, add tofu slices and cook for 5 minutes until golden brown on both sides.
- Serve cooked cabbage stew with fried tofu.

Nutrition:
- Calories: 182 Cal Fat: 8.3 g Carbs: 27 g Protein: 5.5 g Fiber: 9.4 g

Kimchi Stew

• Preparation Time: 10 minutes | Cooking Time: 25 minutes | Servings: 4

Ingredients:
• 1 pound tofu, extra-firm, pressed, cut into 1-inch pieces
• 4 cups napa cabbage kimchi, vegan, chopped
• 1 small white onion, peeled, diced
• 2 cups sliced shiitake mushroom caps
• 1 ½ teaspoon minced garlic
• 2 tablespoons soy sauce
• 2 tablespoons olive oil, divided
• 4 cups vegetable broth
• 2 tablespoons chopped scallions

Directions:

• Take a large pot, place it over medium heat, add 1 tablespoon oil and when hot, add tofu pieces in a single layer and cook for 10 minutes until browned on all sides.
• When cooked, transfer tofu pieces to a plate, add remaining oil to the pot and when hot, add onion and cook for 5 minutes until soft.
• Stir in garlic, cook for 1 minute until fragrant, stir in kimchi, continue cooking for 2 minutes, then add mushrooms and pour in broth.
• Switch heat to medium-high level, bring the mixture to boil, then switch heat to medium-low level, and simmer for 10 minutes until mushrooms

are softened.

• Stir in tofu, taste to adjust seasoning, and garnish with scallions.

• Serve straight away.

Nutrition:

• Calories: 153 Cal Fat: 8.2 g Carbs: 25 g Protein: 8.4 g Fiber: 2.6 g

African Peanut Lentil Soup

• Preparation Time: 10 minutes | Cooking Time: 25 minutes | Servings: 3

Ingredients:
- 1/2 cup red lentils
- 1/2 medium white onion, sliced
- 2 medium tomatoes, chopped
- 1/2 cup baby spinach
- 1/2 cup sliced zucchini
- 1/2 cup sliced sweet potatoes
- ½ cup sliced potatoes
- ½ cup broccoli florets
- 2 teaspoons minced garlic
- 1 inch of ginger, grated
- 1 tablespoon tomato paste
- 1/4 teaspoon ground black pepper
- 1 teaspoon salt
- 1 ½ teaspoon ground cumin
- 2 teaspoons ground coriander
- 2 tablespoons peanuts
- 1 teaspoon Harissa Spice Blend
- 1 tablespoon sambal oelek
- 1/4 cup almond butter
- 1 teaspoon olive oil
- 1 teaspoon lemon juice
- 2 ½ cups vegetable stock

Directions:

- Take a large saucepan, place it over medium heat, add oil, and when hot, add onion and cook for 5 minutes until translucent.
- Meanwhile, place tomatoes in a blender, add garlic, ginger, and sambal oelek along with all the spices, and pulse until pureed.
- Pour this mixture into the onions, cook for 5 minutes, then add remaining ingredients except for spinach, peanuts, and lemon juice and simmer for 15 minutes.
- Taste to adjust the seasoning, stir in spinach, and cook for 5 minutes until cooked.
- Ladle soup into bowls, garnish with lime juice and peanuts and serve.

Nutrition:
- Calories: 411 Cal Fat: 17 g Carbs: 50 g Protein: 20 g Fiber: 18 g

Spicy Bean Stew

- Preparation Time: 5 minutes | Cooking Time: 50 minutes | Servings: 4

Ingredients:
- 7 ounces cooked black eye beans
- 14 ounces chopped tomatoes
- 2 medium carrots, peeled, diced
- 7 ounces cooked kidney beans
- 1 leek, diced
- ½ a chili, chopped
- 1 teaspoon minced garlic
- 1/3 teaspoon ground black pepper
- 2/3 teaspoon salt
- 1 teaspoon red chili powder
- 1 lemon, juiced
- 3 tablespoons white wine
- 1 tablespoon olive oil
- 1 2/3 cups vegetable stock

Directions:

- Take a large saucepan, place it over medium-high heat, add oil and when hot, add leeks and cook for 8 minutes or until softened.
- Then add carrots, continue cooking for 4 minutes, stir in chili and garlic, pour in the wine, and continue cooking for 2 minutes.
- Add tomatoes, stir in lemon juice, pour in the stock and bring the mixture to boil.
- Switch heat to medium level, simmer for 35

minutes until stew has thickened, then add both beans along with remaining ingredients and cook for 5 minutes until hot.

• Serve straight away.

Nutrition:

• Calories: 114 Cal Fat: 1.6 g Carbs: 19 g Protein: 6 g Fiber: 8.4 g

Lightning Source UK Ltd.
Milton Keynes UK
UKHW020631170822
407428UK00006B/60